The Animal Penis Book

The Animal Penis Book

A comic filled journey of nature's weirdest genitals

William Meadows

ISBN: 9781078239189

Contents

Introduction

Have you ever been at a party, a bar, or some work function and overheard someone regaling a crowd of people with a fantastic story? You see everyone laughing and nodding along while they speak. You want that kind of attention yourself but find your brain has failed you in remembering even the smallest interesting fact. This book was created with you in mind. I have spent months researching the world's most interesting, unique, and entertaining facts nature has to offer; from the four hooked knife penis of the Llanos Mosquitofish, to the twenty-seven nippled shrewish short-tailed opossum. With this book you will experience a curated and comic laden journey of nature's best penises, vaginas, and sex facts.

I love learning new information and find myself running down rabbit holes on the internet to find them. As a technical writer and educator by day, I find that the most interesting facts are often ones that are super relatable. Everyone has seen a koala, right? But does everyone know that koala as a species are infected with chlamydia and have two penis heads? That's the kind of thing that really hits people, that the cute sleepy animal is really a bi-headed walking STD factory.

This book is a mixture of about 50% animal penises and their horrifying backstories, 30% animal vaginas, with their twist and turns, and the last 20% is about that manic sex lust that some species have. Just so things don't get too repetitive, these fun factoids are evenly distributed, and backed up with hand drawn comics and the real story of why something would have a knife penis.

Marine Flatworms

In case you have never heard of the marine flatworm before, it is a ribbon like, underwater sea creature. They live in the ocean and sport a vibrant purple and orange coloration, featuring an outer bright yellow or white rim of color on their sides. They have a close cousin you might even be familiar with, the tapeworm; a parasitic variety that lives inside the digestive tract of other animals. What you might not imagine about these guys is they are hermaphroditic. This means they have both male and female sex organs.

This multi-sexed feature makes it a lot easier to survive and reproduce. They are not concerned with finding an opposite flatworm to mate with. All they do is scour the local area for literally any other worm of same species. Then, like a dirty drunken 1:00 am tinder hookup, they have themselves a fight.

They begin by circling one another like two out of the three musketeers. Sneering at each other they start drawing their swords, pulling out their penises while they stare deep into each other's eyes. The time-honored ritual of penis fencing has begun. Yes, they fight with their penises. It is a sexual combat to determine who can impregnate the other flatworm. The winner is the one who stabs the other with their penis and runs away unscathed.

You see, being a mom is hard. And yes, being a dad is also hard, but being a mom-dad hermaphrodite flatworm is like the hardest. That is why making the other flatworm pregnant and avoiding that fate is very important. It takes a large amount of extra energy to make babies, energy better spent on keeping oneself alive.

And these fights are not gentle either, as they can last for up to an hour. Their piercing and sometimes hooked penises can gouge large holes in a flatworm. It is also possible for both parties to 'lose' the duel and each become mothers at the same time. Traditionally, the most successful flatworm is the one that can compete in a long series of these fights before succumbing to motherhood. In the end, the flatworm produces hundreds of eggs that hatch a mere ten days later, the lifespan of these animals ranging between 3 weeks to 4 months on average.

The Water Boatman

Lurking around the shores of freshwater inlets and stagnant ponds worldwide, lives a tiny insect called the water boatman. Coming in around the size of your thumbnail, it sports a mild brown or sometimes black coloration. This inconspicuous little bug happens to prefer a steady diet of plant matter.

The water boatman's life isn't particularly busy, so he spends most of the day playing fine music. He does this to attract the love of a nearby lady. For as we all know, the true way to lady boatman's heart is not through lavish bug gifts - but through song! You might be wondering how does a bug play music, good question.

The lusty bug begins its one note ballad by vigorously rubbing its penis upon its ribbed abdomen. This generates an incredible 100 decibel noise. This sound is about as loud as walking by a busy nightclub on a Friday evening. The vibrations are so loud in comparison to its body size, that pound for pound it is the loudest creature on earth. Thankfully they do this underwater, so we only hear a tiny fraction of it. Lady water boatman absolutely love the vibrant sounds of underwater penis violin and will flock towards its music.

Like whales in the ocean whose songs can be heard from great distances, the water boatman uses his grand penis dirge to attract far away mates. The boatman with the loudest penis is sure to attract more bug ladies and produce more offspring - furthering his loud penis genetic line for many years to come.

Llanos Mosquitofish

Evolution is a strange mistress. Sometimes it's so crazy, it might seem like a mistake was made. What's important however, is that whatever twists and turns are encountered, the animal has a better chance at reproducing. This generally means that a species over time becomes more survivable and longer lasting.

Some animals evolve harder shells, or better eyesight, or even camouflage to blend into its local environment. Unfortunately for the llanos mosquitofish, Mother Nature crafted something a little different. That is because this unassuming tiny fish - has a four hooked, knife penis...

Why?... why is that a thing you might be asking?. How come this fish needs that kind of unsheathed dong weaponry? What could possibly warrant this evolutionary track? Well, most females of the animal world only want to date the largest and biggest males. Regrettably for these lady fish, the preverbal grocery store is filled with overly aggressive and tiny fish suitors. To combat the constant barrage of tiny fish sex, the female llanos mosquitofish evolved a large fleshy vagina blocking mass. This mass stops the smaller less well-endowed fish penises from entering.

This brings us back to the hooked knife penis. For actual procreation to occur, the large male fish must use his *tool* to open up the passageway. This involves a bit of stabbing, jabbing, and sawing but eventually will allow entry to the female's vagina. Since the large male has the appropriately sized tool for the job, he is able to succeed where other smaller fish have failed in their lust.

These little barbed knifed penis fish live in east central Mexico and sport stunningly bland brown scales, but they don't let that get them down.

Kangaroos

We have talked a lot about various penis-ed animals up until now, so it might be time to talk about some vaginas. Let me introduce you to the kangaroo. We all know and love this Australian hopping marsupial, but did you know these gals have three vaginas? Yes, three vaginas and two uteruses as well. While the entry point (cloaca) is a single opening, the kangaroos confusing internals split off into two side vaginas and a central vagina. The side vaginas pass sperm up and into one of the two uteruses which sit happily above the entire vagina cluster, while the central vagina is for actually birthing more kangaroos - pretty standard stuff really.

This unique set of vaginal equipment allows the kangaroo to be in a disturbingly constant state of child production. Including rearing, birthing, pregnancy and nursing. A female kangaroo could at the same time: have one uterus unoccupied and awaiting a sperm donation, another uterus in production creating a new joey (baby kangaroo), have another freshly birthed joey inside the pouch nursing milk, and a youngling skipping next to mom wondering why nature has such a weird sense of humor.

The production cycle will even halt itself if one of the joeys spends too much time in the pouch. Kangaroos have the ability to pause a pregnancy. Pausing will cause the developing embryo to stop developing at around 100 cells, giving the mother a break until the pouch is available for a new occupant.

The female kangaroo also gets some time off if the weather is bad. Well, more specifically if there isn't enough food to go around. When the dry season hits food such as grass will become less available. This lack of food causes the male kangaroos to start shooting blanks. The females will also halt their current pregnancies to save their unborn babies from starvation.

Female Squid

Imagine you are swimming through the water with eight legs twisting and fluttering around. You are a female squid whose interests include eating, not being eaten, and darkness. Really you are just the goth chick from Hot Topic. Off in the distance you see a handsome male squid. This is great because the ocean is very big, super deep, and it's difficult to find a good man.

Mr. Squid sees your lithe twisty from and thinks, "*o my god its time!*", as it has also been a while for him too. Jetting fluid out your back ends, two squid forms rush towards each other. You both meet and stare longingly at one another. Mr. Squid slowly reaches downwards with one tentacle and grabs some sperm from within his own body. Staring deeply into your squid eyes he rubs it around your mouth where it slightly burrows into your skin. What?... Why?... It burrows??

Yes! You see, squids don't have vaginas and most male squids have nonfunctional penises. To combat this problem the male squid creates a spermatophore. A spermatophore is a capsule of sperm with a barbed delivery system. When embedded into the female squid's skin, it releases sperm over time. Shortly thereafter she will become pregnant. There is even a recorded case of a spermatophore embedding into a women's mouth after she ate some under cooked squid.

A female squid can have multiple spermatophores from many males embedded at once. Sometimes however, this method doesn't result in a pregnant squid. If the eggs do not fertilize normally, the squid will grab a handful and hold them to her mouth area. This gives the sperm an opportunity to release immediately nearby the eggs to allow fertilization.

After the hard part is over, the squid mom will round up all the fertilized eggs and spew some homemade jelly around them. This jelly protects the eggs and allows her to place them in nice comfortable hidden areas, like under a series of random rocks.

Sugar Gliders

The sugar glider is a big eyed, flying squirrel looking marsupial. While appearing similar to their squirrel cousins, the primary difference comes from how they birth their young. Sugar Gliders like all marsupials, have a pouch for their babies to live in after exiting the womb. This pouch is a cozy and warm location in which the baby will stay for around eight weeks. Afterwards they are ready to venture outside mommy's belly tent.

What you might not expect from these fuzzy flyers is the bifurcated penis. Bifurcated meaning their penis starts off as a single shaft and then splits into two distinct penis head bits. Now I say head bits because their penis can best be described as looking like two earthworms fighting to the death. Except they are joined at the hip, not looking like a normal penis head, as you might be used to

Now I know I didn't mention this before with the kangaroos, but this two headed penis business is actually pretty common among marsupials. Because again, the number of vaginas seems to range between two to three. You can imagine how having two business ends of a penis could help for getting a two vagina-ed female pregnant. If you think about it, it all makes sense really.

Where things start to get a bit weird is the placement of their testicles. It is above their penis, completely opposite most mammals. Where things get much worse is their penis comes out of their anus. Well, it comes out of their cloaca, which is their one stop party shop for excrement and sexual stuff. God, nature is gross.

Hyenas

They laugh, they cry, they enjoy the full complement that life has to offer. Such as eating animals alive starting from the butthole. Hyenas really are a magical creature that can only be described with phrases like, gross, that's disgusting, and why does she have a penis? These spotted, laughing, cat-dog monstrosities sport one of the world largest clitorises, which happen to look exactly like a penis.

Now you might be saying at this point, doesn't this get confusing? How does one tell the two sexes apart in the field? If both members of this species have a penis/pseudo-penis looking thing dangling between their legs, it is extremely confusing. For centuries we thought that Hyenas were hermaphroditic. And unlike most mammals, the females are about 10% larger and much more aggressive. Often a researcher would track and study a male Hyena for some time, then suddenly find out it was a female after it started nursing its cubs.

Speaking of cubs, hyenas are the only mammalian species that lack an external vaginal opening. This is because the labia has also fused together to form a makeshift scrotum, with the clitoris poking through to form the penis like appendage. What does that even mean? It means that they have to urinate and give birth through their clitoris/pseudo-penis. Let me reiterate - they have to pass two-pound cubs through their clitoris, which will almost certainly rupture in the process. This leads to a high level of mother hyenas dying during their first pregnancies. Additionally, about 60% of cubs suffocate in the one inch diameter birth canal.

If the cubs and the mother manage to make it out of the birth process alive, things get worse for the weaker cubs. Baby hyenas will begin to attack each other almost immediately after birth. This results in about 25% of all hyenas dying to sibling rivalry. The good news is that if a mother hyena makes it through her first pregnancy, she will almost certainly be fine for the next one.

Male Hyenas will spend quite a bit of time shadowing the females they are interested in. Passive males have a greater chance of success when trying to reproduce. When the female is ready and in heat, she will choose one of the males who has been courting her. Since the female anatomy is so odd, there is a zero percent chance of unwilling participation. When ready, the female retracts her clitoris into herself and allows the male to delicately insert his penis into hers. Among humans this might be called docking to use another phrase. Everything after that is pretty normal actually.

Bean Weevil

This unassuming brown beetle ranges in size between a grain of rice and a small grape. The bean weevil lives most of its life inside a seed. Being a granivore, they eat seeds and grains for sustenance. As the name entails the Bean Weevil loves a good legume. Sporting longer mandibles and a pudgy snout, this weevil might even be considered cute.

They are not cute! They are sexual monsters. The bean weevil is one of those "what the hell" animals. When a mommy bean weevil and a daddy bean weevil love each other very much - he whips out his long mace like barbed penis and obliterates her vagina with it. This vaginal destruction is aimed with the sole purpose of making the female Bean Weevil physically unable to have sex again, or at least personally unwilling. Either way the goal for the male is to make sure his sperm is the only sperm she will ever carry. This allows his genetic line to be the only kind that gets pushed forward.

Now this may all sound horrifying... because it is; but the good news is that this sex can make the female bean weevil live a little longer. There are two types of male weevils; those who want to have sex early in life, and those who want to have sex late in life. For some reason the late in life weevils have a special chemical in their semen that increases the lifespan of the female. This magical ejaculate allows the lady weevil to live an average 18.7 days as compared to their 17.9 day normal. This may not seem like a lot to us, but to an insect its quiet a healthy boost - around 5 years of human time. So I ask you, would you be willing to brutalize your vagina to live 5 years longer?

Cuttlefish

These rather funny looking octopus faced cephalopods, are one of the coolest animals you will ever see. They kind of look like a Cthulhu monstrosity, but like fish sized instead of leviathan. Their skin contains color changing pigment sacs that rapidly adapt the cuttlefish exterior to blend into the environment. They are even able to flicker these sacs between colors to appear almost electrical. Regardless, the big takeaway is they can change the way they look on demand.

This is good because not all cuttlefish are created equal. Some are rather larger and a bit more aggressive. Others are tiny and are not really looking for a fight. When it comes to cuttlefish mating habits though, the bigger and meaner you are, the more lady fish you can woo. Not because they are super into your size or attitude, just that you can keep other males away by looking tough.

This is where the color changing aspect comes into play. The big bad mean cuttlefish are on the lookout for rival males and try to scare them off. They will let the females hangout because they are attempting to put the moves on them. What is a young aspiring boy cuttlefish to do? If you said dress up in drag and pretend to be a girl, you are correct! With their ability to change color on demand, the smaller male will change his skin pattern to match that of a female cuttlefish. This allows him to get close to the real lady cuttlefish and start the second act of the drag show.

After he has passed by the gaze of the larger male cuttlefish, the young male will place himself between the female that interests him and his rival. Then he will change just the side of his body that the female can see into the male pattern. This attracts her attention and they will begin to copulate without the larger male's notice. This technique allows even the smallest and weakest cuttlefish to win out in the mating game by being crafty.

Sharks

Believe or not, when the male shark is interested in a female, he will lovingly follow her around for many days to begin the courtship, trailing behind her and avoiding all food in order to impress the lady shark. I'm just kidding, these are sharks... he bites the shit out of her and tries to roll her over for access. Now to be a little more specific, these are more love bites and not full force. But it is very obvious to tell if a lady shark has had sex recently. Alas, the whole affair is forced for the female shark. Her only real protection is to hide in the shallow waters, where it is physically more difficult to flip a shark over.

Not that you needed any more reasons to be afraid of sharks; but I'm just going to be upfront about this one... they also have two dicks. They are called claspers for some pretty obvious reasons. Once the male shark has flipped over and grabbed a hold of the lady shark with his mouth, he inserts one of his claspers into her cloaca. The clasper is armed with a spur or barb that allows the sharks genitals to stay put during the underwater sex fight. This is important as having sex underwater is very difficult. There is nowhere to leverage yourself for pushing. Hence all the biting, clamping, and dick hooks.

Shark sex is just about what you would expect from these undersea murder machines. The good news is sharks don't really feel pain like we humans do. They don't have the same receptors, and sort of just act on instinct when their version of pain goes off. Fortuitously, female sharks are larger and have tougher skin than male sharks. This helps them to deal with the nagging problem of unwanted male advances.

Barnacle

One of the things you learn in life is sometimes you find the strangest things in the most unexpected of places. Take the barnacle for instance, it is an underwater creature that permanently attaches itself to hard surfaces. You might have seen some on rocks near the shoreline or attached to the underside of ships. What is possibly the only interesting thing about these unmoving creatures is that they have the largest penis to body size ratio in the world.

It turns out if you are a completely immobile creature, it helps to have a big dick. The barnacle's penis can grow to up be to 8 times the size of its body. This is important because the barnacle uses his massive wang to play Marco Polo with nearby partners. Like a blind man delicately tapping his cane on the sidewalk, the barnacle searches for a friend. When the barnacle finds this friend, he gently spews semen all over the body of his new mate.

If the barnacle is out of luck and cannot find anyone within penis distance; he will attempt to use sperm-casting to further his genetic line. Although it might sound like some kind of black magic for semen, it's really the fine art of tossing sperm in the air and hoping it impregnates someone. Except the air is water and the someone is a barnacle somewhere in the nearish vicinity.

What is even weirder is that their penis length is almost entirely dependent on how rough the local water is around them. If they live in a calm and easy tide zone, their penises will grow to their maximum length and thin out. Alternatively, if they are in rough seas, their penises harden and reduce to a thicker, stronger, more resilient appendage. Anyways... next time you are down by the beach and you see a bunch of rough looking, sad barnacles, remember that they actually have it pretty good.

Blue Whale

We just finished talking about the barnacle, which has the largest penis to body ratio. That's all well and good, but how about we introduce the world's biggest penis overall. Ladies and gentlemen, stand back, stand aside, and keep your head down for god's sake. Here comes the title holder himself, the *BLUE WHALE*!

A bit much? Probably... but the blue whale sports on average a 7-foot, 10-inch penis. Now granted, the penis is pretty thin in comparison to most penises. Its diameter is somewhere between 12-14 inches, but it weights around 400 to 900 lbs. That is literally enough dick to kill a man if it fell on him. That's not all! Supporting the massive man killing penis, are two 100-pound testicles that can pump out an impressive 5 gallons of semen during climax.

As we all know, these blue whales are around 100 feet long and are the largest animals on the planet. They weigh somewhere along the lines of 300,000 pounds, so it's pretty expected that they would hold the record for the largest penis. Little is known about their specific mating habits. We do know that they are a non-monogamous species and females will have sex with many males. This helps to up the odds of becoming pregnant. When the baby is born, it is on average one quarter the length of the mother, making it larger at birth then most other animals are in their prime. These whales can enjoy swimming around the world oceans for up to 100 years. Their only real predators happen to be humans and large packs of orcas.

Hermit Crabs

In the world of the hermit crab, life is all about your home. They are a crustacean like many others, but they need to find residence in discarded shells. These shells are hard to come by and many crabs will take some time to hollow out the insides for extra space. Possibly to add a new bathroom or remodel the kitchen - that kind of stuff.

The problem is their entire life hinges on the fact that they have a house. If a hermit crab is without a home for more than 24 hours, they are very likely to die from exposure and drying out in the sun. That doesn't sound so bad when you have your house stuck to your back, but what if you wanted to get lucky? What if you meet a nice lady crab and wanted to show her a good time? Well I've got good news and I've got bad news.

The bad news is you are going to have to leave your house partway. You can park your house as close to hers as possible, but at some point, you are going to need to stick your dick through her front door. That is not a euphemism, the hermit crab must literally put his penis into her shell opening and deposit a spermatophore on her or nearby. This means that if there are house robbers in the near vicinity, they have a great opportunity to rob you out of house and home. Rival hermit crabs that are looking for an upgrade in real estate, will watch for mating pairs and attempt to snag a new house. To make matters worse, if your house is super nice, even the lady hermit crab might try to take it from you. There is no justice in this world.

The good news is nature has worked in your favor. Over time, evolution has crafted some big dicked hermit crabs to deal with this particular situation. If you have a long enough penis you don't actually have to sneak that far out of your house. This allows you to rest comfortably inside your home and sling your crab meat through her front door without worry of being robbed. As you might imagine, sex is probably the scariest part of a hermit crabs' entire existence.

Thankfully for them, copulation lasts only for a few second up to a minute.

Angler Fish

If you are not familiar with the Angler Fish, they are a deep sea, dark brown, toothy monstrosity. They are notably famous for a bright, glowing appendage that sits atop their head. It can act as a lure that brings prey close to their horrifying mouths. This lure is very important in the ever-present darkness that lurks far below the ocean's surface.

What is particularly special about this species is the female is 40 times the size of the male. Her goals in life include not moving much, murder, and attempting to lure a male partner to procreate. To help find a potential mate in the vast underwater dungeon that is the deep ocean, she unleashes a chemical attractant into the water that acts like a homing device for males. The males look almost nothing like the female Angler Fish. Not only are they much smaller, they sport huge eyes and nostrils that help in locating her through the darkness

Once the female has been found, the male will swim up to her and bite down on some part of her body. From this point forward he will never let go for the rest of his life. He has now transitioned into a parasite, taking in nutrients directly through the female and her blood stream. His mouth, eyes, and face will fuse into the female's skin and he will essentially become a tumor on her side. His only function from this point onwards is to be a pair of gonads, to provide sperm on demand when the lady Angler Fish is ready to fertilize her eggs.

Multiple males can attach themselves to the female, and up to eight have been found attached at one time. It is very important for the male to find a female as quickly as possible as they are truly born for the task. The males are ineffectual hunters and cannot survive on their own. They can only hope to find a girl to latch onto otherwise they will perish.

Pigs

Of all the creatures that are in this book, pigs are probably the one that people are most familiar with. So much so that we have all kinds of sayings that are related to them. Pigging out, acting like a pig, sweating like a pig. Did you know that pigs don't even sweat? That's why they roll around in the mud, so that the evaporating water from the mud can cool them down. It also acts like sunblock for their sensitive skin.

What you might not know about male pigs is that they can continuously ejaculate for up to 30 minutes at a time. Now this record was made with the use of a gloved hand. In real life scenarios pigs only have sex for around five minutes but can last as long as twenty. During this time they are able to pump out up to 400ml of semen. Just remember that a standard can of coke is 330ml, so take a moment to drink that in. It has also been noted that if you stop the procedure of helping the pig get off, they will become angry. So the next time you see one of these barnyard playboys, remember not to start anything you don't plan to finish!

Black Widow

We all know the tales of the black widow. She is a dangerous spider and is consumed with evil desires. This venomous creature is known for killing her mate after they bang it out. But the story is a little deeper than you might know. First, there are like 30 different species of these guys, and only a small handful of them actually do the post coital snack thing. Secondly, almost all documented cases where the male was eaten, were observed in a laboratory environment where the male could not escape. Third, it almost feels like he deserves it after you know a little of the back story.

The thing is male black widows are pretty much dicks. They are much smaller than the females but that doesn't stop them from causing havoc. Their main goal in life is to have offspring, but first they need to find a partner. He will spend quite a bit of time roaming about searching for a mate via pheromones. These pheromones are placed on web strands that his female mate has anchored nearby. This smelly lifeline will lead the male straight into her lovely home.

At first he will hang out and get the lay of the land, taking stock of her house which she has spent countless hours building. When ready to shake things up, the male will proceed to cause havoc. He cuts the lines and strands of her silken bungalow and begins to bundle it up with his own silk. This move is calculated as it allows him to hide the very same pheromone trail that he followed. Balling up as many entry points into the inner sanctum as possible so no other males can follow his lead.

When he is ready to get it on, the male will then construct a sperm web. This creation is like an artist's paint tray, because he will ejaculate onto it like Bob Ross spreading titanium white in preparation for a canvas. Once satisfied with the consistency or color or whatever it is spiders care about, he will smear and spread the semen all over his palps. The palps are the little appendages near his mouth that are syringe like in structure. Once appropriately applied it's time for business! The spider lets loose and will dance his way up to the female. This dance is a special dance that lets her know he is ready to begin mating.

Prepared with his 'jizz' hands... palps, he finds her genital opening on her abdomen known as an epigyne. One by one he inserts the palps into her while desperately trying not to irritate his lover. After the semen is placed into the semen receptacle inside the lady spider, he will attempt to make his escape. Most species do this successfully, but some will end up as a sacrifice to the spider gods and become an after-sex snack.

Damselfly

The damselfly is a rather similar cousin to the dragonfly. They sport slightly slimmer mid sections and have wings that fold alongside the body. They are a fantastic messenger of nature, as their presence is a good sign that a local body of water is not polluted. They only drink the finest of non-bottled waters and cannot tolerate anything less.

When preparing to mate, a male damselfly will approach a female and fly on top of her. He begins by grabbing her on the back of her neck using his tail. The end of said tail has what could be described as a claw machine attachment. This mechanism allows him to hold her with a perfect grip, as the claw end matches the back of her neck like a mold. Each subspecies of Damselfly has their own neck/claw device system. It is theorized that this helps to stop interbreeding attempts.

The female Damselfly is totally into this neck grabbing. When ready she will place the end of her tale near the end of the male's abdomen, where his penis resides. This will create an almost heart or wheel shaped outline. They have to make this odd posture because the females' vagina is located at the tip of her tail. To increase the difficulty of the whole operation, the sperm creation organ is at the very end of the male's tale. Which means there is a bit of distance and pump priming that needs to happen first.

Step one is for the male damselfly is to clear out the old sperm from the ladies last mate. These girls happen to be just as promiscuous as the guys. Using his penis the male scoops out the inside of her semen receptacle (yes that's a thing, bugs are weird) by pumping back and forth using his pipe cleaner like penis. Once completed he will begin to push all the semen from the tip of his tail all the way to the beginning and push it into her.

Damselflies practice delayed pregnancy. This means she might not fertilize her eggs at the moment that the male ejaculates. To ensure that his sperm in the material is used, and isn't removed by a rival, the male plays the waiting game. He will continue to hold onto her until she actually lays the eggs. This proves to the male that his genetic line will continue. After the lady finishes egg laying, he will fly off and attempt to find new love elsewhere.

Bees

Bees are our buzzing friends often found floating about colorful flowers during springtime. Their black and yellow color makes them very distinctive in the bug world. As you might know, these worker bees are all female and work together to feed the hive. Yet these bees do not provide the hive any reproductive services, they leave all that business to their queen.

As far as bee sex goes, it is important to understand the monarchy's role in procreation. While the worker bees dutifully go out and find pollen for the hive, the queen sits back and makes an unreasonable number of children. Those children grow up to be one of three types of bee; a worker bee (female), a virgin queen bee (female), or a drone (male). When these guys grow up from larva and turn into real adult bees, they begin their careers. The drones (male) are born without stingers and do not gather nectar or pollen. Their only goals in life are to get laid or die trying.

This leads us back to the virgin queens. When they are ready to become breeding queens they take wing and fly outside the hive. They make their way to a breeding ground called the congregation area. These are naturally occurring areas where bees keep coming back to in order to reproduce. They are somewhere between 5-40 meters off the ground, around 30-200 meters wide, and fairly protected from the wind.

Awaiting her at the location are thousands of male drones, buzzing excitedly for a chance to further their genetic line. These drones come from all over the local area for this opportunity. This in turn allows greater genetic diversity for the soon to be non-virginal queen. They are all very patient though, as they will ignore her until she is fully within the congregation zone. Once she crosses that line however, it's game time.

As she flies into the breeding area, she is immediately swarmed by male bees desperately diving and trying to attach themselves to her. Only 1 in every 1000 males will ever get the chance to procreate with the queen. They fly around making a bee comet hovering through the sky. Seriously, that's what it's called. Once a drone does manage to attach onto her abdomen, he immediately inflates his endophallus. His penis inverts from inside him and unrolls into her opened sting chamber. That is not a euphemism. This whole process takes around 1-2 seconds on average. He immediately becomes paralyzed and ejaculates his bee load with such explosive force, you can hear an audible popping noise when he gets off. This causes his penis to rupture and tear from his body while he shoots away backflipping because of the energy. What's left of his penis stays inside the queen in an attempt to stop the leakage of his cargo. He dies almost immediately afterward.

Ducks

Ah, ducks. We all know and love these feathered quacking creatures. They are in our cartoons, old people love to feed them, and in general they seem like pretty peaceful guys. Well, you are wrong! Duck sex is a horrific ordeal for everyone involved. You cannot trust these things farther than you can throw them. All duck sexual anatomy is just a continuing series of evolution trying to avoid rape.

Male ducks are very aggressive and have been trying to force the mating card for a long time. They are also equipped with a counterclockwise cork screwed penis. Female ducks needed a way to control the situation at least somewhat. So they evolved a clockwise corkscrew vagina to make it harder for the men to penetrate them. This had mixed success. Some male ducks' penises started turning the right direction. So the ladies evolved branching vaginas. Some ducks have dead end alleyways in their vaginas to confuse the duck's penis. Now I say to confuse the duck penis because the male must unravel his dick inside of the vagina, like blowing up a balloon in a tube. Yes, ducks are weird.

Not all is horrible in duck land. Some lady ducks actually want to mate with particular males. A female duck who has found a partner can straighten out her body and lift her tail in just the right way so that her vagina straightens out. This makes it much easier for her chosen suitor to unravel his penis down the correct passage. But if she is being forced, she will fight and tighten up making it more unlikely that the attacker will fully penetrate her. Although many ducks mate monogamously for the season, if there are not enough females to go around multiple ducks will gang up on a single female.

In other interesting duck penis news, at the end of the mating season the male's penis will shrivel up and lose most of its mass, in some cases just falling off. This will reduce it to around 10% of its previous volume which will begin to regrow to full size again in the spring.

Opossums

Just in case you didn't know the difference between a possum and an opossum, it really all boils down to location and looks. True possums have a furry tail and live around the New Guinea and Australia region. Opossums have a bare tail and live in North America.

Commonly known for the ability to play dead the opossum is a medium sized, white, gray, and black marsupial. This means like all our other pouched animal friends, that they have a two headed dick and multiple vaginas. Old news these days. Who cares about that kind of thing at this point in the book! What is really interesting about the opossum is that they are only pregnant for 12 days!

Once that male possum finishes spraying his love juice into one of her two uteruses, and it fertilizes some eggs, it's like the twelve days of Christmas. Except you get burdensome childcare as a present instead of something good. I say that because possums can have up to 20 babies at one time. Sadly only about half actually survive, but those are the breaks. It is a tough journey at 12 days old from the vagina to the mother's pouch, which has only 13 nipples to speak of. You might have noticed that 13 a lot smaller than the number of possible babies (20). If you are a baby possum you better get here early, as seating is limited. Baby possums are about the size of a dime when they first born and are innately able to work their way to the pouch without any help.

When the babies are done with the nipple and pouch life, they begin to work their way upwards and become a true pain in the ass. Well... ass, back, head, they occupy the entire upright part of mother's body, and a bit on the sides. They ride her like an overcrowded pony who works too many jobs to put up with this kind of shit. But she is a good mom and lets them see the world from her shoulders.

Dolphins

Dolphins love to swim in open waters, avoid long walks on the beach, and are highly intelligent social creatures. What you might not know about these quick, shimmering, water dwelling mammals is they are sexual miscreants. Dolphins have a dark sexual underbelly that make even the most notorious playboy fraternity guy squeamish.

Dolphins get started young. Before reaching sexual maturity, dolphins will engage in many non-reproductive sexual behaviors. This includes touching themselves (masturbation), touching others (second base), and homosexual contact (college) - all before they are old enough to vote. They are so into this kind of thing, that some dolphins will even mate off species.

It's not all fun and games though! Dolphins do have a dark side. Many male dolphins will work in small groups and form alliances that force female dolphin to have sex with them. Up to 14 males will work together to harass a female. Running into her, slapping her with tails, corralling her so she stays near. This high amount of group sex and forced mating leaves dolphins as prime targets for STDs and STIs like genital warts. When she gets pregnant and has a calf, if a male from a rival alliance finds her baby there is a good chance he will kill it. Her only real protection against this is to mate with as many different alliances as possible. This will ensure that no one actually knows who the father is.

Alligators

Masters of lurking in the depths within some fetid swamp in Louisiana, alligators are some of the best ambush predators in the world. They take most of their meals on the go. Specifically, by dragging them deep underwater where they drown while being chewed to death. These skilled wielders of surprise don't just utilize it for murder, they also sport a permanently erect hidden bungie penis.

Contemplating what that sentence means can bring forth some troubling imagery. In short, alligators are another animal that has a cloaca. The triple threat pee, poop, sex hole that many reptiles, bird and marsupials have. In the horrid depths of the alligators' sewer portal, the rock-hard reproduction baton awaits. Instead of being filled with blood or lymph like kangaroos or ducks; the alligator's penis is filled with hardened collagen. That is what gives it the permanent morning wood look.

At a moment's notice the alligator can rapidly deploy his penis outwards through the cloaca. While there is no direct tendon or muscle pulling it forward, the shape and nearby tension of other muscles launch the rocket out. There is, however, a rubber band like tendon on the tail end of the penis that pulls it back in like a spring when the other muscles relax.

The actual courtship of alligators is done in the usual way. A bit of swamp bellowing and tail thumping in the water. The male alligator tries to lure in a potential mate from the surrounding wilderness. Once appropriately attracted they mate only seasonally, with a laborious 30 seconds of alligator sex. Tipping the scales of what is even reasonable.

Clownfish

They are bright orange with bands of white and black, and can be found in the warm shallow waters around the Southwest Pacific Ocean, the Red Sea, and the Indian Ocean. You probably know about clownfish from Finding Nemo or because you like sea anemones. Either way they are a rather interesting type of fish because they tend to live a dual life. Clownfish are one of the few species that can transition between the sexes.

All clownfish are at first born male and are fairly small and submissive. They live in a dominance hierarchy like many animals, with a mating pair of male and female at the top. The lady fish is the head of this particular organization, unlike much of the animal kingdom. When it is time to breed she will develop a clutch of eggs and prepare a clean area in the sand for them.

Up to 1500 eggs can be produced at one time and placed in their new home. The male will come over at this point and complete the fertilization by spraying semen in the immediate vicinity of the eggs.

At this point the female clownfish will leave, and the male will gently take care of the eggs by fanning them and protecting them. This fanning greatly increases the survivability of the eggs by pushing fresh water over the eggs and keeping particulates off. The baby Clownfish will hatch somewhere between 6 to 8 days later without any real maternal oversight.

When the female of the group dies, things start to shake up in the colony. The current dominate male will rapidly begin his sex change operation to occupy the spot of top dog. While the next runner up in the submissive male category will grow in size and become the new vice president of clown fishery. All pretty standard stuff really.

Neotrogla

Neotrogla are a type of lice. Well, cave lice to be specific. They live in Brazil and subsist on a steady diet of bat shit. They are about the size of a flea, so very, very small compared to the other animals in this book. Surprising to no one, while great for fertilizer, bat shit isn't exactly full of nutritional value. In order to combat this impressive lack of sustenance, these cave lice developed a new paradigm. The males evolved to have the vaginas, and the ladies get to chase after them with their penises. It's all very modern and new age.

The standard gender roles are a little reversed as you might expect. The females are extremely aggressive in searching out mates, while the males are fairly selective. When mating, the females will mount the male from behind and penetrate his genital opening with her gynosome (penis). Her penis will swell and deploy barbs to prevent unwanted removal. This will begin the process of sex, where semen and nutrients are removed from the male through her penis. Like a sexual straw she drains him of life-giving material. This love making can last up to 70 hours.

Neotrogla might have evolved this method to help mitigate the female's energy burden from being pregnant. Trying to forage enough energy for a new mother would require eating a significant amount of bat poop. The male helps out by spending most of his life building up nutrient supplies and semen, later providing it for his mate like some kind of sexual lunchable. There have even been instances of females mounting and sucking the juices from juvenile males who were too young to reproduce, all in the name of an easy meal.

Phallostethus

An interesting name for what at first glance seems to be a rather dull tiny fish. Gently swimming in a stream, this fish was found in the waters of Vietnam. As you might know from its Greek root this fish has something to do with a penis. This little guy is from the family of Priapium fish. These fish all sport a rather humble yet menacing penis (priapium) under their chins! Not only do the males have their equipment out and about, but the females have their sexual opening under their mouth as well.

When mating the male fish will move near the lady fish to form a 'v' like structure. Face to face they stare forward together as the male uses his penis like appendage (priapium) to clasp onto her. It has a saw-toothed attachment made for this purpose. Once engaged this way, he transfers his sperm into her allowing for internal egg fertilization. This is actually rare for fish in general.

Now I have been skirting around that fact that a penis is not a priapium, but for illustration purposes it helps put the mind at ease. I did that because it's particularly odd to explain that the priapium has on one side an anus, and on the other side the genital opening, and an additional saw-toothed hook knife thing. Really a lot of this is hard to believe and I understand that, so please go look it up yourself - it's insane.

Bonobos

The bonobo is our closest cousin in the animal kingdom. Looking like a chimp in structure, it's their temperament and attitude that distinguishes them from their warring tree dwelling neighbors. Bonobos live in a much more peaceful society than the chimpanzee. They manage this atmosphere of contentment through the time-honored tradition of 'Banging it out' whenever tensions get high.

Bonobos have a lot of sex. They do this for a variety of reasons, but the main one is to avoid violence. It is very common for tension to elevate when evaluating a promising new food source. Like determining who will get first dibs at the plum tree for example. This is a perfect time for Bonobos to show a little love and work out the physical tension. Bonobo sex comes in all forms: female to female, female to male, and male to male. I put the lady sex at the beginning of this list because bonobos also live in a matriarchy. Researchers have noted female Bonobos practicing tribbing (clitoris to clitoris rubbing) to help smooth out problems. Lead females will work out their tension together for around 20 seconds. In that time there is a measurable heart rate increase, facial flushing, shrieking, and clitoris engorgement. All the usual signs of pleasure and orgasm. They also participate in kissing with tongue, and oral sex.

Males and females will of course procreate, and they do it more or less with everyone. They also practice some amount of face to face mating; looking at each other during the act. Humans are the only other primate that also performs this style of intimacy. Since there is so much inter-tribe mating, the males don't exactly know which kid is their kid. They decide not to invest time in taking care of the young because of this lack of insight. This leaves child rearing up the mothers.

As mentioned before, Bonobos live in a hierarchy where females take a dominant lead. Some males are able to obtain better positions because of their mothers. High ranking Bonobo females can 'lend' some status to their male offspring, making some of the males higher in status than some of the low-ranking females. A good bonobo mom uses this power to help their male children find suitable mating partners. Some vestiges of this practice can even be located among humans.

Leopard Slug

Squirming delicately on trails of mucus, the leopard slug, Greek name Limax Maximus (literally meaning big slug) is fairly easy to find. They range between four to eight inches long and are covered with spots. These spots are the reason they are called leopard slugs. Hailing originally from Europe, you can now find these guys pretty much all over the world.

The leopard slug is a hermaphrodite (like all slugs), containing both male and female reproductive organs. Unfortunately for them, they are unable to do the deed with themselves. They need to find a friend to join in the festivities. When ready to do so the slug will begin to excrete a special tasting ingredient into their slime trail. The human equivalent of walking down the street while throwing skittles on the ground, waiting for someone that is hungry/horny enough to follow it into the bedroom. This method can take some time as these are slugs we are talking about. Once the appropriate slug suitor has been found, it starts off by biting the original slug's ass to let it know it has arrived. They then make their way up the nearest tree or other tall thing nearby. Once above ground level they begin to mate.

Leopard slug sex is a lot like a ballet mixed with a lube wrestling competition. For about an hour the slugs will wrap and writhe around each other. Intensely getting closer and entwining themselves. This action repeated over and over produces a thick mucus. When they are ready, they will let go of their branch or high place and begin sliding downward on a thread of mucus. Free floating above the ground, they unleash their penises from the side of their head. The penises are almost the size of the slugs themselves and are a translucent electric blue color. These too begin to wrap around each other and fan out to create a spherical ball of penis. It might even be described as 'flower like'. This is when they transfer their sperm to one another, allowing their eggs to become fertilized.

Afterward they will separate and fall from the mucus line, sliding away to lay eggs somewhere safe.

The Anaconda

I think we can all agree that snakes are weird. The anaconda is like the final boss of snakes as far as I'm concerned. They are absolutely huge and would strangle the life out of a water buffalo if given the opportunity. All of that aside, they are complete freaks in the sheets.

When it is time for making baby anacondas the female will start releasing pheromones for the male snakes to find. These smelly pheromones linger on the ground where she has been, and float through the air. She will more or less stay in the same place while she awaits the onslaught of snake flesh. Typically this will be in a shallow lake or stream or marsh. When a male snake wanders through the area and smells the booty call signal, he will make a bee line that direction.

Upon arrival he is greeted by a writhing mass of snake scales and wrapping flesh. He has successfully found the breeding ball. A mess of horny male snakes (up to 12 including him) are desperately wrestling around her, squeezing and stimulating her in an attempt to mate. They are each trying to position their cloaca beside the females and stimulate her with their tiny mating claw. When she is ready, which can take up to a month, she will open up her cloaca. Whoever the lucky snake is on top will be able to mate with her. He will deposit his sperm, and a sperm plug into her. The sperm plug is there to help keep his sperm in while she is wiggling around, and to stop rivals from getting an opportunity as well. This is only a small inconvenience as the rivals will try to squeeze or scratch at the female to pop it out.

In the end many males will have mated with her, but it is normally only the strong or crafty that do so. She will slither away and find a nice safe place to sunbathe for 6 months while her babies grow inside of her. Anacondas are one of the few species of snake that grow and fertilize the eggs internally, giving birth to live young. She will not eat during this time, as she will become slow and fat with all her young inside of her. This could cause her to be injured while hunting and hurt her procreation success. She will end up losing more than half her body weight in the entire process of bearing young.

Snails

Ah, snails... nature's way of shaming you for walking barefoot at night. They can be found pretty much everywhere, and some are even the size of your hand. Snails are a type of mollusk that live both on land and in water, although you are most likely to see these guys hanging around in your garden, eating your tomatoes or favorite flowering plants.

Like most creatures in this book, their sex life is one filled with battle and strife. Snails are hermaphrodites and sport both male and female sex organs, very similar to slugs. As we have discussed earlier being pregnant uses much more energy and is a slow way to pass on one's genes. So the snail is another example of a creature that tries its best to avoid having children, while inflicting that curse on another. When a snail is hunting for a sex partner it must do so by taste and smell. Snails are essential blind and can only see if something is dark or light. Once a snail has tasted a slime trail of a new potential partner, it begins its quest.

Things are actually fairly cordial when the snails meet. They begin by rubbing up on each other, tasting and feeling with their tentacles. This lasts for thirty minutes or so in order for the snails to get acquainted. When ready to actually mate the snails stab each other with a love dart. The love dart is a small, hardened, hormone filled injectable needle. Its goal is to lower the other snail's innate semen repellent chemicals within their body, furthering the chance that they will get their partner pregnant. They "shoot" the dart by inflating a sac that is attached to its base, and lodging it into the other snail's skin.

After stabbing each other, the snails will deploy their penises from the side of their necks, each snail inserting theirs into the others genital pore (read vagina). If their love dart did its work correctly, they will fertilize the others eggs. If there were some issues with aim, then the natural semen repellent will ward off the pregnancy. These love darts not only decrease the sperm resistance in their body; it also shortens their lifespan around 25%. Un-darted snails live around 60 days.

Cats

Cute, cuddly, and slightly annoyed by your very existence, cats have been a staple of human society for thousands of years. Existing since the time of the pharaohs, they have even kept company for many famous writers. Ernest Hemingway's cats were well known for their extra toes (polydactyl cats).

Like all living things, the call of sexual maturity brings new passions, yowling into the hot summer night. Some breeds, like the Siamese, reach sexual maturity as early as 4 months old and produce up to twelve offspring. With numbers like that, you can see how quickly the cat population could get out of control. Although not the intended purpose, I'd like to think nature has devised a way to help. Male cats seem to have a terrifyingly barbed penis.

The barbs cover almost three quarters of the cat's penis. They are small and backwards facing yet hard because they are made out of keratin. That is the same material as your fingernails. These barbs are painful and very unpleasant for the female cat, but they serve many purposes.

Like some terrible BDSM fantasy the barbs make it much harder for a female cat to get away from the male. It is also very painful for the penis to be removed, leading to some after sex ass whooping from the female cat. However, evolution has made the barbs entirely required for making babies.

The lady cats have an estrous cycle and go into heat for 5 to 7 days every month. During this time her body is actively encouraging her to look for a mate, unlike a menstrual cycle where a human female can look for a mate at any time. The sad part of the tale is that lady cats cannot produce an egg without the males barbed penis. The barbs must be painful enough to stimulate their release. Her body is hard wired to trigger the release of eggs based on this painful interaction.

So if you are lying in bed at night and hear the high pitched growl screaming of a cat, it could be one of two things; it was either a vicious territorial dispute, or some cat just yanked its barbed penis out of her. If it was the yanking, she is now in the processes of biting the shit out of him.

Dogs

Even man's best friend makes an appearance in this book. While they might not be as horrifying as some of the other animals that have been featured, dogs have a few special traits that we need to discuss. I am willing to bet that almost everyone on earth has seen a dog's penis. If you haven't you are either five, or you are a terrible shut-in. If you are five I'm very impressed with your reading level, but you should probably put this book back where you found it.

The actual penis is usually hidden within the prepuce - the fuzzy hair covered bit between the dog's legs. When excitement occurs, a bright red penial shaft can poke forth. Generally though, dogs will not get erect until their penis is within the vagina of their mate. If this sounds impossible and confusing, bear with me.

When it is time to make some puppies, the male will mount the female and assume the position. He manages to get the flaccid penis into the lady dog through diligent use of his penis bone. That's right, dogs have a bone in their penis and it's called a baculum. Many placental animals including primates have one, except for humans for some reason.

Once within the female, the dog's penis engorges rapidly. This engorgement fills both the shaft and the Bulbus Glandis (the knot) at the base of the penis. When inflated the knot helps to lock the dogs penis inside the vagina. At the same time muscles within the vaginal wall clamp down on the knot, forming a strong seal tying the two animals together. They will remain this way until after the male has inseminated the female. While the deed might get done within two minutes or so, it can take up to 20 minutes for everything to release itself. Trying to force the dogs apart can result in extreme damage to the animals. So please just let things happen naturally if you find yourself in this situation.

Shrewish Short-Tailed Opossum

Try not to get upset, but if you remember earlier on in the book we discussed opossums already. Luckily, there are many breeds of opossum and they are not all created equal. That previous opossum was particularly interesting because of the short gestation period of its young (around 12 days). Here I bring you probably one of the most interesting animal facts in this book, almost certainly the most interesting opossum fact! I'll lay it out straight for you, this animal is the most nippled animal in the world.

That's correct, the shrewish short-tailed opossum flaunts an amazing 27 nipples on its tummy. Covered in dull brown fur, this opossum is native to Brazil, Argentina and Paraguay. What's also unique about them, is the lack of a pouch for their young to grow up in like other marsupials. Their babies still have to make the same arduous journey from the vagina up the belly, unlike kangaroos for example, whose spoiled children get their own tummy house to live in. These poor suckers have to keep climbing and latch onto one of the 27 nipples or die trying.

Imagine the life of that mother opossum! You just gave birth to over a dozen of these tiny bastards, and now they are hanging onto your nipples like dollar store Christmas ornaments. They will eventually move away from the nipple when they grow up. This is when the mother will realize they just move onto her back. Being more than just an emotional burden at this point, they weigh her down physically as well. Opossums are a strange group of creatures...

Argonaut

Don't worry if you have never heard of the argonaut before. It is an octopus that happens to like making a shell around itself. It can leave the shell as it pleases but would prefer not to. The shell is primarily used as a mechanism for staying neutrally buoyant when floating in the ocean. They manage this by trapping gas bubbles inside the shell and filling it over with the octopus equivalent of cement. It doesn't offer much protection from predators though as it is extremely thin, giving it an almost paper like appearance. This look has also given them the nick name of Paper Nautilus.

As cool as the argonaut might be, only the female lives the house life. They are also much bigger than their male counterparts, so much so that the males are fairly worried that they might be eaten by them. So when it comes to sex, the males have developed a unique strategy. They rip their penises off and have it swim after the female. This detachable penis which is really a modified tentacle that carries sperm. It will swim up to the lady Argonaut by itself and embed in her mantle. She uses the penis tentacle (hectocotylus) later when she wants to fertilize her eggs, which she also places inside her shell.

When Argonauts were first discovered the hanging penises attached to the female where thought to be a parasitic worm. Only after further investigation into the life cycles of the Argonaut did we learn the truth. Argonauts are also featured in literary works such as Twenty Thousand Leagues Under the Sea. This book gave rise to the idea that they use their tentacles as sails, to travel the oceans. They don't.

Pandas

You know them, you love them, they are difficult to breed. Introducing the Panda! This black and white vegetarian bear has found itself on the short end of the endangered stick for some pretty obvious reasons. They seem to have a particularly hard time having sex, and an even more difficult time raising children. They also live on a steady diet of bamboo, which does not provide a lot of nutritional energy for an animal who digestive track was built to eat meat. This makes them one of the least suited animals to still be on earth. But if you are cute enough humans will try their damnedest to force you to have sex.

Pandas can be found in the remote mountain sides of central China, residing in wet bamboo forests. Out in the wild they live a very solitary life, preferring to stay away from others. This doesn't help when they actually go into cycle and are ready to mate, because pandas are only sexually active for a very short window of time. This window being 24-72 hours once a year. Like the same amount of time law enforcement give kidnapping victims to survive. And if you think the female panda is running around desperate to find love, you would be wrong. Her best calling card is to rub anal secretions onto nearby trees and hope to god someone is nearby to smell that she is ready to get down. It's the human equivalent of writing "fuck me baby" on a post card and throwing it in the trash.

Believe it or not, this actually works sometimes and on occasion too well. If there are multiple males, she will climb up a tree and wait for the most dominate one to sort out things on the ground. When ready she will slide down and present herself in the most available way possible. She will push her butt high in the air while keeping her tummy on the ground. This is necessary as pandas have the worlds smallest penis to body ratio and need all the help they can get. He will then mount her and quickly work up to orgasm. At this point the male grabs hold of the female and sits down, pulling her up and onto him, desperately trying to work every inch of panda inside for a snowball's chance in hell of getting her pregnant.

In captivity things somehow manage to get worse. There is apparently something special about rubbing your anus on a tree out in the open that just can't be mimicked in a controlled setting. A team of researchers and zookeepers desperately keep an eye out for signs that the she is in her kidnapping victim pregnancy window. When they have confirmation, their next job is to hope to god the captive male is in the fucking mood. Apparently pandas need bonding time to really get to know each other. In situations where that wasn't enough, they show the pandas videos of other pandas having sex. They show them panda porn.... And even then, they still won't have sex most of the time. This is why pandas are endangered! That and humans messing up their habitat...

Polar bears

Stepping into the ring at somewhere between 500 to 1300 lbs., the polar bear is the largest land carnivore in the world. They spend much of their time hunting their favorite food; any seal stupid enough to get eaten by a land animal. These guys will range hundreds of miles in search of these stupid seals. Polar bears are experiencing a bit of an issue with their habitat as the sea ice they roam on is melting. Caused by global warming and greenhouse gas releases, polar bears seem to be in a bit of peril. Also their dicks are breaking, and we are on the hook for that too.

It would seem that some of the pollutants from the manufacturing of pesticides and solvents are giving polar bears osteoporosis. Osteoporosis is a condition where your bones become weak and brittle. These pollutants have worked their way up the food chain and into the dumb seals that the polar bears love to feed upon. Once the seal is gobbled up by a somehow extremely quiet and sneaky 1000lb predator, the pollutants have made their way into the bear.

Just like dogs and many other mammals, polar bears have a bone in their penis. If that penis bone happens to be too brittle and breaks during sex, that polar bear will be unable to perform further to help make new cubs. This will lead to a steady decline in the overall polar bear population in the arctic.

Whiptail Lizards

Living in the southwestern United States and northern Mexico, the whiptail lizard is a rather magical lady. She is colored in tan-orange scales with radial stripes running from head to tail. She comes from a land where there are absolutely no man lizards, and she wouldn't need one anyways. This old girl manages the phrase 'go fuck yourself' with astute clarity and accuracy. The whiptail lizard is able to reproduce all by herself.

Whiptails are able to clone themselves via the process of parthenogenesis. Parthenogenesis is the act of developing an embryo from an unfertilized egg, the same thing that happens in plants. This feature can allow them to take over a bunch of land with just one individual. No longer are they restricted by the need to find an appropriate mate like some species do. They are also susceptible to having their entire species whipped out due to a lack of genetic diversity, such as in cases of plague or changes to the environment.

To get the whole reproduction party started, whiptails still engage in some mock mating behaviors with other members. This would include mounting. Since they are all female though, they have been given the nickname "lesbian lizards" for their trouble. This mock mating is thought to jump start the process of parthenogenesis. Afterwards she will lay up to four eggs which will hatch around eight weeks later.

Otters

The playful jesters of the sea and nearby bay inlets, everyone loves otters! They are adorable and they hold hands so they don't drift apart from their friends. They love to eat and enjoy life, so much so that they consume around 25% of their body weight per day. But what they don't tell you in otter school is that there is a disturbing underbelly to these floating furry feasters. They need to eat so much food, that there has been recorded instances of male sea otters stealing babies from their mothers. They will hold the pup underwater until the mother pays a ransom and gives him food. If she isn't fast enough the poor baby gets to drown.

When it comes time for otters to make baby otters... things get worse? When trying to find receptive females, the otters come off as playful and happy. When the lady finally accepts the advances, he quickly leaps on top of her and begins biting the shit out of her nose. When she submits to him he forces her head underwater into a mating position. Many otters die because of these wounds or even from drowning while mating. This does not deter the male otter however, as they will continue to have sex with the corpse, repeatedly.

Absent otter females, the males have been known to have sex with other species. There was a recorded instance of a male otter capturing a harbor seal pup and having sex with it. The otter managed to kill it in the process. Death was not going to pause the otter from returning and having sex with the body for days afterwards. Male otters are sickening sexual deviants and are undeserving of your love. Feel free to still like female otters and baby otters, before they grow into detestable sexual monsters.

Elephants

Tall, majestic, and wonderfully smart creatures, elephants bring a great sense of poise and class to any book about animal genitalia. That is why with great reverence and dignity I wish to tell you about their four-foot-long, 60 pound, prehensile penises.

In case you do not know what prehensile means, think of your fingers. It can do that, but in like all directions. It's like a monkey's tail actually. Able to bob up and down and curl even into an s shape. They can use their massive penis to even scratch their tummies when it itches. At this point you might be asking why they would evolve such a dangly prehensile penis. Well, elephants are huge and it's very difficult to actually do any kind of humping per say, so they do none of it.

They rely on their penis to worm its ways in and out of the lady elephant's vulva. Now you might have noticed I didn't say vagina, that's another problem here as well. The elephant's actual vagina is like 3 meters deeper inside the elephant. You can imagine it's somewhat difficult to get the right juices flowing where they need to go. The good news is that elephants have an 18 week estrus cycle, so they have a bit of time to try to get things working. When they do succeed, elephants are pregnant for the longest amount of time on earth. After 650 days they will produce a huge blind baby elephant weighing about 150 pounds.

Naked Mole Rats

What is best described as a burrowing ball sack with legs, the naked mole rat is one of those creatures that can make you question everything you believe in. They are mostly blind rodents that have no hair. They live almost their entire lives underground, and for some reasons are highly resistant to cancer. They can survive for up to 18 minutes without oxygen and can numb themselves to pain. They seem almost like a super animal. All that aside though, their males produce some of the most pathetic and lack luster sperm on the planet.

Naked mole rats live in a colony structure underground. The head of the colony is the queen mole rat. She spends much of her time getting pregnant, being pregnant, and making sure no one else can become pregnant. She is the biggest cock block you would ever have the unfortunate luck to meet. Her being around the colony causes everyone in it to not want to have sex anymore.

The queen is able to suppress the reproductive organs of everyone except the few breeding males. She does this either by simple aggression or a unique chemical in her urine. Non-breeding males produce lower numbers of sperm, and have no desire to mate. Only when completely removed from the colony will they regain their natural libidos.

Even the breeding males have had to go through this period of sexual repression, and it has led to some of the most useless semen ever found. The sperm have messed up heads, sometimes two, they are nearly all immobile or unable to swim straight. The sperm also have significantly lower amounts of energy stores available for their journey.

You might be asking at this point "isn't this a problem?" Well, if just you and two of your buddies are the only ones having sex with the queen, it really doesn't matter what is wrong with your sperm. They have never needed to evolve better, stronger, faster sperm to compete within the vaginal tract. Everyone in the breeding group get a guaranteed appointment with the queen for procreation duty. So even if only 1% of their stagnant inept sperm can move, that is enough.

Koalas

Huggable, fuzzy, and cute, the koala is a super cool critter that lives in eucalyptus trees. These guys are a member of the marsupial group so say it with me kids; two penis heads, two vaginas, blah, blah... we've heard it before. BUT, these ones are special and slightly different you see. Instead of being born like a normal creature by passing through one of the vaginal passageways, these guys elected to bust through the middle of their "vaginal "cul de sac". This tearing of the wall leads to the urogenital strand, which allows the baby to exit out the cloaca. Thrilling.

After growing up the young adult koala might find itself in a unique sexual landscape. Most of its species is infected with chlamydia. Some populations experience up to a 100% infection rate. While not exactly fatal chlamydia can lead to several bad side effects such as blindness and incontinence. Additionally, the koala population is currently dealing with its own retrovirus issue. In short, that means the koalas have AIDS. This of course leaves the koalas susceptible to other infectious diseases and cancer.

The big problem is these viruses are being passed from mother to offspring almost immediately. Eating eucalyptus is difficult and requires a specific gut microbiome. To accommodate her child's needs, the mother feeds her baby a little bit of poop. This allows her to transplant a little bit of her stomach flora into the child. Now I know you are not a doctor, but you are right, that's not good for stopping koala AIDS.

The treatment for helping the koalas is not a good option. To cure them of chlamydia you need to provide them with antibiotics. But if you do that, it will disrupt their sensitive gut microbiomes, a sad catch 22.

Echidna

Hailing from Australia where all weird things seem to congregate is the echidna, Nature's dumpster fire. They have been described as a cross between an anteater and a porcupine. Sitting quite low to the ground and covered in spines, echidnas are fascinating marsupials. Uh oh, did you hear the magic word again.... marsupial, which must mean two vaginas and two dick heads. Normally you would be 100% correct but in this case it has FOUR dick heads. Here you were thinking you had nature figured out.

The echidna sports a sprinkler head for a penis. It looks somewhat like a disfigured flesh colored flower. What is super interesting however is that when the echidna ejaculates, it only fires semen out of two heads at a time. Leaving the other heads to rotate in for the next ejaculation. Speaking of ejaculate, theirs is also fascinating. Their sperm likes to bundle up in groups of 100 or so. They swim together in a tight ball which helps increase speed and mobility. It's kind of like watching a group of cars drafting together to reduce fuel cost. Scientists assume this trait evolved because echidnas' mate indiscriminately and sometimes in rapid fire. The echidna with the best sperm teamwork is probably going to pass on its genetics. Did I mention these guys also lay eggs? They are one of only two mammals that have this special power. The other animal being the platypus, another one of god's science experiments.

Bed Bugs

Bed bugs are probably the creature that most people would least like to find in their home, other than a man-eating tiger. While they may be disgusting and a horrifying blood sucking parasite, their sexual behavior is somehow much, much worse. When it comes to love making, these tiny brown bugs follow the motto of 'stick it to em'. Sorry, I'll be clearer, they stab each other through the stomach with their razor sharp penises.

Basically their dick is a hypodermic needle. The male will sneak up on a lady and jab his penis into her thorax, injecting semen into her bloodstream. As the blood makes its way around the tiny bugs body, some of it find a way into the ovaries, resulting in fertilization. This method of copulation is called traumatic insemination and is extremely bad for the lady.

These wounds are an open door for infection and can lead to death. Male bed bugs will also mate with other male bed bugs and pierce their abdomens as well. In the bed bug world attraction is based on size, and they will mount any partner regardless of gender if they are big enough. In general, the females are larger than the males so it's not a bad rule of thumb to jump on any bigger bug. But when bed bugs feed they greatly increase in size and change to a more red color. This can be enough to confuse the non-discerning bug eye and encourage a male on male piercing.

In the end we can all agree that it sucks to have bed bugs in your home, but it might possibly suck more to be a bedbug.

Porcupines

Waddling through the forests of North America lives a prickly rodent known as the porcupine. Legendary for the spiny quills that cover almost their entire body, the porcupine is a modern wonder. Not like a building or a great architectural marvel, but like I wonder how the hell they manage to have sex and not spike the crap out of their genitals. Maybe you have never thought about that before, but here we are... asking the difficult questions.

Well, it all starts with the female getting in the mood. Again, just like pandas, this happens only once a year around September. During the other parts of the year her vagina is usually closed with a membrane since it is used so infrequently. This in the mood period lasts for a desperate 8 to 12 hours, where she must attract a mate from somewhere within the nearby forest. Generally porcupines live solitary lives so her mileage will vary.

Not to worry, however, because like most mating problems, these kinds of things are always resolved with foul smelling mucus and other bodily secretions. These secretions are supplied by her vagina, which she will rub onto trees. The smell acts like a homing beacon for males to find. At this point she will wait in her tree and watch patiently as suitors arrive. If a lucky guy gets there a bit too early, as is normal, she will make him wait below on a lower branch of the tree. This gives time for more males to show up and fight over her. In general, the stronger male will win the fight, leading to stronger babies.

When the time is right, the remaining male will get the female in the mood by spraying urine at her. If this displeases the female, she will scream violently at him, which honestly seems appropriate. Otherwise she will present herself by raising her tail up and onto her back, while lowering her quills. This give the male a precious few inches to work in that won't quill his penis... much. This method is one of the few in the animal kingdom that gives the female control over the penetrative elements of mating.

Moths

They are like the little brother that never gets any attention, the ugly duckling of the flying flappy bug world. Once a beautifully colored exotic looking larva - many moths manage to turn into a rather dull brown winged creature that exists purely for sex. Some moths such as the Creatonotos Gangis, like to spice things up. They have an incredible Cthulhu-esque appendage that flares outwards from their butt. Many had assumed that this was their penis (including the author of this book). Now we know it's truly a 'feather duster' for perfuming pheromones into the air, which is even more interesting.

There is actually a full group of both moths and butterflies called Lepidopteran that have these appendages. The official name for the appendage is coremata or 'hair-pencil'. This group notably includes both Monarch butterflies and Luna moths. The pheromones they release act as both an aphrodisiac and a tranquilizer for females. It also helps to keep other males away by being a repellent.

The coremata are rapidly deployed from the inside of the moth and unravel outwards filled by air or lymph, similar to blowing up a balloon. The pheromones are deployed and pushed into the air by this action. If the female is nearby she will notify the male she is attracted by wiggling her antenna at him rapidly. From there onward the bug sex is pretty standard. He passes her a sperm filled ball with his penis and she stores it in herself for later. Either moving on to find another mate or to produce eggs.

Sea Turtles

We have all seen the videos of hundreds of baby sea turtles desperately clambering over each other trying to make it into the sea, climbing from the sand out of the buried pit their loving mother left them in. Being eaten by seagulls and other predatory animals on their hair-raising journey to survive like ten minutes in this damn world. Have you ever wondered how exactly that all was set in motion?

When the weather starts to warm up, and it's around the right time of the year - female turtles will find their way back to their original birthing grounds. Probably with the thoughts of "well if I made it out of that hell hole alive, surely the next generation can do it!". Already awaiting them will be a horde of mating age males swimming around in search of an available female. They tend to operate on a first come first served basis. Luckily for the males, the females don't seem to mind who fertilizes them, just that the job gets done.

This means it's kind of a race to be the first male to jump on the ladies back and hold on for dear life, like a cowboy riding a bull, but with other cowboys trying to knock you off. The mounting male will use his clawed flippers to hold into the front of the female's shell and his tail to hold onto the end. The claws are very sharp and will cut the female sometimes, leading to gashes and visible injury. From here the male will whip out his extremely bulky and long penis - measuring out to be almost half of his body length. He penetrates her cloaca and grips tightly for a long ride, sometimes lasting for up to 24 hours. The length of stay is mostly due to keeping other rival males off of her. This gives his sperm the most amount of time to actually fertilize the eggs. This isn't without some cost though, as other males without mates will bite and claw at him while he rides out the storm.

When the sexual rodeo is completed, they will separate and find new partners to begin the process again. The female will mate with many males over the breeding season, as she has multiple clutches of egg to bury into the sand, like some terrible buried alive Easter egg hunt.

Chromodoris Reticulata

I know the name isn't exactly helpful here, so I'll just tell you these guys are an underwater sea slug. I can already hear you moaning, "not another damn slug", but these guys are even cooler than all the previous slugs and snails and whatever. These guys have multiple detachable penises! Now as we both know by this point, slug like creatures are hermaphrodites. They have both the key and the lock when it comes to genitals. Except these guys expect to lose their key after unlocking the door. Like walking home from the bars late at night and throwing your keys into some random corner of your house.

After mating in the usual slug way through semen exchange from one partner to another, the slug's penis falls off and a new one starts to regrow in its place. The growth is really just the uncoiling of a deeper down segmented portion of the entire penis. Now this takes a little bit of time - somewhere in the 24-hour range, but overall not too bad. In the laboratory environment there was a lucky candidate who managed to make this penis transactions three times in a row (with the mandatory 24 hours break in between)

Now if you are asking why would this even be a thing? Well these guys like many other species we have talked about, have backwards facing barbs. These barbs make it much harder to remove the penis. So just leaving it in your partner and walking away is an option that these guys are ok with. It could also be used for scraping the remaining slug semen from the last dude, out of the female side of their partner. Giving theirs a better opportunity to be the winning sperm.

Ribbon Eel

As a sub part of the moray eel family, the ribbon eel might be a little overshadowed in your eel knowledge. These ribbon eels come in different colors ranging from midnight black, to yellow with blue highlights, to pure yellow. In the past we had thought these different colored eels where different species. After some examination it turns out that they are all the same species. The only difference is that as they age they change the color of their skin. It transitions over time, but that is not the only thing that transitions.

As the ribbon eel works its way into old age it turns female. It would seem that all ribbon eels are born male and they all start off as that midnight black color. Later they work into mature males as a yellow blue, and finally become female that can produce young. Interestingly enough, these ribbon eels have a very hard time living in captivity. They only make it around a month on average with the longest ever living about 2 years. If you wish to see them in the wild you can find them ribboning around in the Indian and Pacific oceans hiding among the coral.

Antechinus

This tiny rodent looking mammal is the most sex crazed animal of any that we have talked about so far. They also happen to be marsupials, so we all know what that means at this point... two vaginas. Yet as a seemingly new development these guys have a normal single headed penis. These little guys live in Australia and are about the size of your fist. The males live an unusually short life brought about because of that aforementioned sex crazed attitude.

Reaching sexual maturity before they are a year old the Antechinus will just make it into the mating season. At this point their body goes into sexual overdrive and releases large amounts corticosteroids. They will stop producing any more viable sperm and their testes start reducing. So for them it's about time to try to get out every last usable drop. This means a nonstop sexual marathon that can last for a few weeks.

Each individual sexual encounter can last up to 14 hours at a time. This means no sleeping, no eating, no grooming... nothing! The enormous lack of self-care leads to the male Antechinus literally falling apart from broken down muscles and skin diseases, over time becoming a patchwork, disgusting mess. Near the end of the male's life most females will completely avoid them because of their sorry state. Soon after these used up sex machines will fall over and die, bringing new meaning to the idea of living fast and dying young.

Red Velvet Mites

Kind of looking like a cross between a spider and a red pincushion, the red velvet mite is one of the greatest love Casanovas around. Even though they are a member of the arachnid family, these guys are willing to go the extra mile to attract a suitable mate. Found mostly in dry locations like deserts, they also happen to enjoy living in wood piles and decaying leaves. This is important because to be a real bug bachelor, you need to build a house - and these locations are littered with materials.

Now these guys don't just go building a love pad with nails and sheet rock, no, no, no! They cobble together their love nest with good old silk, semen, and whatever is lying nearby, the tried and true building method of their fathers, and their father's fathers! These materials might include grass, sticks, and mud, but most importantly semen. For the finishing touches on his new love shack, he weaves a finely crafted and intricate silk walkway leading towards the entrance.

When a lady mite wanders by and sees this well-crafted home, it really gets her in the mood. To seal the deal, the male will be waiting at the end of the walkway doing a lovely dance to try and entice her to come over. If interested, she will walk along the path and work her way into his inviting house. Once there she will locate the equivalent of his couch and take a seat. This is where the magic happens. What she actually took a seat on was yet another bundle of sperm and now she is pregnant. All's well that ends well for the mites, and she leaves happy with the transaction.

BUT, lurking nearby is a jealous, not so good at house building neighbor. Watching for when the owner is away, he will run inside and quickly spread his semen all over the couch area and anywhere a lady would sit. The next time a hopeful female wanders in because of this stunning display of architecture, it will be his genes that are spread and not the original builders.

Humans

I know you are thinking this one is a bit of a cop out, but I encourage you to take a long look at our outstanding human history. We are a people who have waged wars over love. We are a species that build the tallest structures and the grandest objects. Buildings like the Taj Mahal were created as objects of love expressed. We created a globally connected electronic network, where information spans the world in a matter of seconds, yet it's littered with porn. Some members of our species enjoy being hit with whips and yet others like to be the one to do the hitting. The number of people who go to the hospital because of lamps stuck up their asses is far greater in humans than an any other animal.

What I'm trying to say here is that for all the research that was done to write this book, no other animal in all its depravity was quite as deep. Humans are by far the weirdest, kinkiest, most interesting of all the creatures on earth. I think this would be a good point to add something about how it makes us a charming species. Something like it's our love for each other that brings out the best in humanity. But I won't bore you with that kind of sappy writing :D

In all seriousness though, if you are looking for a reason to care about nature, or the planet, or about learning in general - even some of the most benign looking creatures might surprise you for what is lurking under the surface. Sadly, many of the animals we talked about in this book are working their way close to extinction. Animals like the polar bear, the panda, and the koala are having a much harder time procreating and staying alive. This is mostly due to human involvement through pollution and habitat destruction. If you take away one thing from this book, I hope that it's the idea that animals are cool as hell and it's up to us to make sure they stay that way.

Acknowledgements

Writing a book is harder than it looks and there are a large number of people who helped get this thing over the finish line. So, to everyone who has been interested in this idea and wished me the best I thank you.

Thank you to Kevin Parsley for editing the book and making it something that is actually readable.

Thank you to Art Rollman and Ron Meadows for proof reading and catching all those mistakes.

Thank you to Aarthi Kannan for laughing at my jokes, encouraging me to keep going, and being the first reader of almost all the content. Your support made writing this book so much easier.

And thank you (the reader) for sharing your time to learn something about all these animals. Spread these silly facts around and make sure to have fun.

About the Author

William Meadows is a passionately curious autodidact. His career has included working with lasers, teaching teenagers how to code, and creating classes about cloud technology that are taught globally. His dedication to completing goals and helping others is what brings meaning to his life. In his free time, he enjoys reading Reddit and playing video games. He is always experimenting with ways to increase his happiness.

Made in United States
Troutdale, OR
01/25/2025

28318747R00062